Underst

Yanderes and Appeal

KAI WEI

Copyright © 2018 Kai Wei

All rights reserved.

Introduction/Advisory

I would like to thank you very much for taking the time to read this book. *Understanding Yandere Lovers: Yanderes and Appeal* is the third part of the *Understanding* series and is meant to inform and look at the appeals of the character trope known as the Yandere. For those who do not know what a Yandere is, we will be covering it in more depth within the book. I want to make sure you have a thorough understanding of what they are as well as why they may seem attractive to others. Similar to all my books, I want to try and simplify it down as much as possible into easy, digestible chunks that can be an interesting for anyone to read. Please have an open mind to any of the information you may deem as controversial, offensive, or odd as we will be going over topics that may not be part of your everyday life. As a disclaimer, this book does not intend to encourage or accept any actions that one may try or imitate in regards to Yanderes. When you finish this book, I personally hope that you will truly understand how a Yandere works and why you might have an appeal for them.

Much Appreciation
-Kai Wei

What are Yanderes?

Before we begin, we must first understand the Yandere. As an anime or manga fan, you most likely came across or have heard of the term Yandere. On the internet, this term is commonly accompanied by a picture of a girl who seems to have obsessive eyes and probably blood stains on her face. There are different variations and thoughts on what exactly this term means, but in order to simplify it; a **Yandere** is a person who at first seems caring, sweet and innocent, however, they turn to someone obsessive, violent and psychotic often due to their devotion towards their particular love interest. This particular character trope often gets displayed in sudden reactionary tendencies. Although Yanderes are usually depicted as females, they are not necessarily bound to the female gender. Males can also become Yanderes, however, it is quite rare to find one in the wild.

The term Yandere originated from anime/manga from Japan dating back to the 1980s and is a combination of the two words yanderu (病んでる), which means sick, and deredere (デレデレ) which can be described as lovestruck. Although the term had been around for a while, it did not grow in popularity until the early 2000s due to characters in anime and manga. More recently, it became popularized due to the game *Yandere Simulator* by YandereDev. As it grew in popularity, the use of it in common speech had also developed into a versatile term which can be used as a noun, verb or adjective to help describe psychotic love behaviors in other people.

A Yandere's behavior and actions are typically driven by one thing: extreme devotion towards their particular love interest. This can include highly disturbing moments such as murdering others out of jealousy and stemming an unhealthy obsession of keeping their love interest for themselves. In extreme cases, Yanderes are known to kill their love interest in order to keep him or her for themselves. Of course, a Yandere's actions and behaviors vary from person to person. There are different levels of Yandere extremism and one can be more obsessive or more psychotic than the other. It simply depends on their nature and personality.

In regards to age, they typically fall between the early teens and early 30's. This is not to say that Yanderes cannot fall outside of this age bracket. The mentioned age bracket it just the area where most Yanderes tend to form and develop their feelings toward their love interest. When all is said and done, Yanderes tend to stay Yanderes for the rest of their lives.

Since a Yandere's facade is being sweet, cute, and innocent, it can be extremely difficult to identify them in the early stages. You must be aware of their traits and characteristics and become very observant of their particular actions that may give their true personalities away. We will go over these in more detail later in the book.

Understanding Yandere Lovers: Yanderes and Appeal

This is a Yandere

How do Yanderes Form?

As previously mentioned, Yanderes are mainly driven due to their devotion towards their love interest. Although they all have this in common, how one becomes a Yandere is a completely different subject. In this particular case, we will be dividing Yanderes in two groups: Natural Yanderes and Artificial Yanderes. A **Natural Yandere** is someone who develops into a Yandere due to natural experiences and circumstances, typically out of their control. Examples of these would include (but are not limited to): personality disorders, parental abuse, illness and traumatic events. An **Artificial Yandere** is someone who chooses to become a Yandere out of their own free will and develops their traits artificially over time. An example of this would be if someone who vibes with the term Yandere and forcibly changes their personality traits to fit those of a Yandere. Both types are still considered to be Yanderes, however, for our purposes, we shall only be looking at Natural Yanderes, as they will provide us the best insight on how they normally develop and become the Yanderes we know today.

When it comes to Natural Yanderes, there are many causes and reasons why someone can naturally develop as a Yandere. Usually, it is a culmination of these various causes that lead to their development. However, in order to focus on several key points, I will be narrowing it down to only 3 main reasons why someone can naturally develop into a Yandere.

Past Trauma: One of the biggest factors that play in the role of the development of a Yandere is their past traumatic experiences. These experiences negatively takes a toll on their mental states. One such common traumatic experience is through constant child abuse during early adolescence. This encompasses various forms of trauma due to the infliction of physical, sexual, or psychological harm. Another common past traumatic experience is being bullied by others. These experiences in turn, creates negative effects in a person's psychological wellbeing and often leads to mental health issues such as: Anxiety, Depression, Lower Self-Esteem, Dissociation, and constant fear. Now, this is important in regards to Yanderes since mental health issues lie at the core of their very actions and beliefs towards their love interest. A Yandere own anxiety, fear and lower self-esteem leads to their psychotic state. Their dissociation, and depression leads to their constant unhealthy attachment to their love interest. This is the reason why they do what they do. They have to deal with their own mental health issues and it is simply directed towards their particular love interest.

Personality Disorders*: Another big factor that plays in the role in the development of a Yandere is the acquirement of personality disorders. **A personality disorder** is a type of mental condition that often leads to harmful patterns of thinking, behaving and basic interactions. These disorders can be broken down into Groups A, B and C. Group A are disorder that fall under the category of odd and eccentric behaviors such as paranoia and lack of emotional understanding. Group B are disorders that are distinguished by the overly emotional and unpredictable behaviors like through narcissism and anti-societal behaviors. Finally, Group C involves personality disorders that deal with anxiety and fear such as being overly obsessive or dependent. These personality disorders can be acquired through birth or through the environment around them. Yanderes in particular can be born with these personality disorders or are very susceptible at acquiring personality disorders around their late adolescence (Ages: 18-20). In this case, their actions and behaviors towards/for their love interest, tend to be seen as odd or unusual due to their personality disorders. Since Yanderes tend to have one or more forms of a personality disorder, this tends to amplify their actions and love for someone in an extreme way, hence their development as a Yandere.

Rejection: More specifically, initial rejection tends to be a common cause of the rapid development of someone turning into a Yandere. This typically happens when they do not know how to cope with the pain of the initial rejection from their love interest. Due to the influx of various negative thoughts and emotions after a rejection, they go through a state of denial known as a **rejection alteration**. This typically leads to their sudden personality change and their continued pursuit towards their love interest in either an unhealthy possessive or obsessive manner.

As a reminder, these 3 points are not the only reasons why someone can develop as a Yandere. These 3 reasons are just the most common way in which someone naturally develops into a Yandere. Many other factors that were not stated here can affect a person's mental state in a negative way.

*In the section regarding personality disorders, further information can be found here:
[Citation Link] https://www.mayoclinic.org/diseases-conditions/personality-disorders/symptoms-causes/syc-20354463

Above is a form of Past Trauma that can make someone develop into a Yandere.

Tsunderes to Yanderes

As mentioned in the previous section, rejection can play a very important role on how someone can develop into a Yandere. A particular character trope that is highly susceptible to rejection alteration are Tsunderes. A **Tsundere** is an anime/manga slang word that is used to describe a character trait that switches between the two emotional states of hostility and affection. It is usually associated with people who do not know how to outwardly express their true feelings and therefore create a hostile outer shell to compensate their inability to express their affections. For example, someone is considered to be a Tsundere when they display their true feelings for someone by punching their particular love interest.

The reason why Tsunderes are highly susceptible to becoming Yanderes is due to their inability to properly deal with their emotions, especially regarding their love interest. What rejection does is amplify the influx of negative emotions which Tsunderes cannot properly comprehend and deal with the pain since they already had trouble expressing their true emotions. This leads to Tsunderes going to one of two paths.

One path they can go through is called the **Tsundere Maturity Stage**. This is where a Tsundere in a sense, "matures" psychologically as the shock, sadness and the pain of rejection, shapes their current personality and helps them better comprehend their emotions. They understand that it just wasn't meant to be and will slowly let go of their attachment for their love interest and find a new one. Of course, they are still considered Tsunderes and will still act like one, however, they become a more toned down version and can better understand their own emotions towards their particular love interest.

The other path they can go through is developing into a Yandere. When a Tsundere is unable to let go, the only way to they know how to deal with their emotions is to channel it into becoming either obsessive or possessive towards their love interest. This process occurs at a rapid pace, however, it is not instantaneous. It will usually take a couple days for Tsunderes to lament the facts of the rejections. Slowly yet surely, their thoughts will begin to deteriorate and their clouded judgement decides to still pursue the same love interest, hence the Yandere developed actions. Although the main factor for Tsunderes developing into Yanderes lies solely on the individuals base personality, you must be wary just in case you happen to be dealing with any Tsunderes in your life.

Understanding Yandere Lovers: Yanderes and Appeal

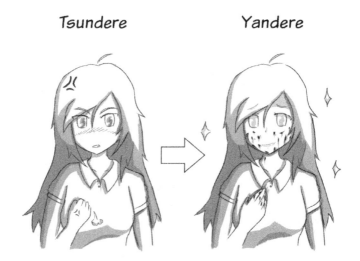

Yandere Types

Yanderes have many different types of quirks and character traits that make them unique. Some Yanderes may be more manipulative. Others might just be plain crazy and really good at knowing your every move. It is impossible to cover all these types because it will vary from person to person via their personalities. Although there are many different types of Yanderes, they do tend to fall under one of two categories: Obsessive or Possessive. As the name implies, **Obsessive Yanderes** are those who obsess over their future together with their love interest and their actions are done to make sure that happens. **Possessive Yanderes** on the other hand, are those whose actions and beliefs are directed towards keeping their love interests as theirs, and theirs alone. Now these two particular categories aren't necessarily separate from each other. In fact, they typically intertwine with one another to make a Yandere. These types may even transition from one to the other, depending on the circumstances and situation[**]. It just so happens that a Yandere may be more inclined towards a Possessive or Obsessive nature, and thus this is how we classify them.

Understanding Yandere Lovers: Yanderes and Appeal

**Disclaimer: Transitions from possessive to obsessive and vice versa, happen very rapidly and typically occur during major life events (typically love related). Such events include breakups, getting into a relationship, etc.

Obsessive Yanderes

Obsessive Yanderes do come in a variety of personalities, however, they tend to have very similar traits. Typically, they obsess over their love interest from afar and often are very good at hiding their aura of intentions. They are usually very shy and have the ability to gather lots of information regarding their love interest. It wouldn't be unusual for them to obsess over you in secret. Some may even have a dedicated shrine or item that they use to worship you.

I guess in an Obsessive Yanderes' mind, they picture the perfect scenario of when you two are together and will take the necessary actions needed in order to achieve it. Some of the actions they may take in order to get closer to their love interest are listed below.

Obsessive Yandere Actions:
- **Stalking their Love Interest**: Obsessive Yanderes have a tendency to follow their love interest from the shadows without being noticed. This is all to feel like they are closer to the person they love. If you have ever felt a presence constantly watching you, that's probably them observing and staying close by.
- **Glorification**: Who else could love their lover more than an Obsessive Yandere? They will often place

their love interest on a pedestal and see absolutely no flaws to them. This creates a powerful drive to worship and adore you, often at an excessive amount.

- **Hiding True Motives:** When it comes down to it, Obsessive Yanderes are really good at hiding their obsessive side, especially to the public eye. From the public's point of view, they might just see a normal person who has a crush for their love interest. This facade is very important to Obsessive Yanderes since it creates less problems for not only themselves, but also for any future issues that may arise in regards to their love interest.

- **Love Interest Research:** They are master investigators. Obsessive Yanderes will typically find as much information as they can about their love interest. From their hobbies to where they work and live. If there was a quiz show about you, there would be no competition (no pun intended).

- **Competition Elimination:** They would never want to hurt their loved one, however that is not the same for others. Eliminating the competition is probably what an Obsessive Yandere is best known for. Anyone who may be seen as a threat of taking you away from them can become target. Many tactics such as manipulation, blackmail and fear may be used against those who are close with their love interest. In extreme cases they may resort to violence and killing.

If you have seen these types of actions from your lover, you most likely have an Obsessive Yandere and must take necessary precautions against them.

Dangers of Obsessive Yanderes

Besides the fact that these Yanderes are deeply infatuated over you at an unhealthy level, the biggest danger of having an Obsessive Yandere is the harm they may cause to those around you. Naturally, since they are obsessed with you, they most likely will not do any harm towards you. They will tend to resort more towards dealing with things that affect your surrounding environment. What this means is that anyone who may seem like they would take their love interest away, will be dealt with accordingly by an Obsessive Yandere. This is especially true against rivals who may be competing against them for their love interest's affection.

Anyone seen as a potential love rival, will usually be dealt with by any means necessary. Even if someone like your close friend has no intention of taking you away from them, this can still be seen as a threat to an Obsessive Yandere. From blackmail to sabotage, an Obsessive Yandere will do anything to make sure that their rival no longer wants to pursue you. In the worst case scenario, their actions may lead to killing someone discreetly in order to get rid of them forever. This is why it is important to keep your friends and family in check whenever you have an Obsessive Yandere.

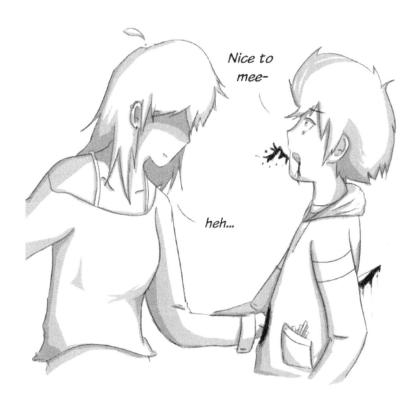

Possessive Yanderes

Unlike Obsessive Yanderes, Possessive Yanderes typically have a more direct approach when it comes to their love interest. They are not afraid to show their affection to you and are known to try and isolate their love interest from other people. Towards their love interest, they can easily show their affection as well as act all cute and innocent for them. This however, is their personality only shown towards their love interest and can easily crumble when they snap. The thing that will trigger a Possessive Yandere to snap and act in a psychotic and violent way is their emotion of jealousy. They are very sensitive especially when it comes to dealing with other people that try to get close to their love interest. Any little interaction with others can set them off and they are not afraid to be confrontational towards other people to tell them he/she is theirs and theirs alone. They of course do this in a calm manner as to not show their Yandere side.

Typically, what they want from you is your undivided love and attention to make sure you never leave them. Some things a Possessive Yandere might do to achieve what they want from their love interest are stated below.

Possessive Yandere Actions:
- **Limiting outside interaction:** Due to jealousy, Possessive Yanderes want to limit any type of

interaction you have with other people. They don't want to lose their love interest and they are not willing to take any type of chance. When other people do try to interact with you, they will make it very clear (whether directly or indirectly) that their love interest is strictly off limits.

- **Making sure you don't leave their side:** Possessive Yanderes say they have to constantly stay by your side for your safety. The world is a dangerous place, so they HAVE to be by your side. I mean else who else can protect you better than them? You don't have the freedom to do things by yourself? I guess it is a sacrifice a Possessive Yandere has to make.
- **Manipulation:** A Possessive Yanderes job is easier when you cooperate and love them. Through conditioning and constant manipulative tactics such as lying and fear, they are able to receive the affection they are looking for without having to constantly force it out of their love interest. For example, you should already know that you are theirs and theirs alone thanks to the constant conditioning efforts towards you.
- **Requesting Lover's Reassurance:** Since Possessive Yanderes are typically insecure, they will constantly ask for some type of reassurance from their love interest. This can come in the form of manipulating/asking you to say that you will always

stay by their side and love them. Sometimes you might just be reassuring them out of fear so that they won't snap and start threatening you.

- **Threatening you for going against their wishes:** Threats come when you are trying to do something a Possessive Yandere doesn't want you to do. They only want what is best for their love interest, so why would you not listen to them? These threats can either be directed towards you or made indirectly by affecting those around you.

Dangers of Possessive Yanderes

Possessive Yanderes are highly volatile and dangerous. They are most dangerous when you are in a relationship with them, since they have that reassurance that you are theirs and theirs alone. The reason why they are so dangerous is because they pose the biggest threat to your life. One wrong move from you and who knows what a Possessive Yandere will do to make sure you don't leave them. Even if you have no intention of leaving them, they may still get sporadic and accuse you of trying to leave them. Any hint or sign that you might be leaving them, and their mood will shift to the worst and start threatening you in various different ways. For example, if your friends are very important to you, then one way they can threaten you is by saying "It would be a shame if something awful were to happen to your friends." In the worst case scenario, when they have no other way of getting you to stay, they may resort to killing you in order to keep you for themselves.

Now don't get me wrong, killing you is the last thing they would ever want to do. They love you so much, so of course they don't want to harm you in anyway. It is only when their love is met with resistance is when they have to make their compromises. Some compromises might include restricting you from going anywhere, or threatening others you know so that you stay. To them, it is all about what will make you stay and love them. Meaningless things, such as your happiness and freedom, will always come second. There really is no other preventable measures besides loving your Yandere.

How to find a Yandere

Yanderes are typically hard to identify, especially in a public setting. They are very good at concealing their true personality and tend to blend in with the crowd due to their **facade form**. Their facade form is a separate personality that enables them to hide their true Yandere intentions from others and have a completely normal one as a facade. This means that in public, they simply look like any other person. In order to better spot Yanderes, we have to look at both look at their physical characteristics as well as their personalities in both their facade form as well as their true Yandere form. Below is a list of things you should look out for in both their facade form and their Yandere forms.

Facade Form

Physical Traits/Characteristics:

- They tend to be physically attractive and innocent looking.
- Typically smiling and can be seen as friendly and approachable.
- Not necessarily the most noticeable person in a crowd.
- Known as being athletic in regards to physique and skill.

- Very fun and bubbly aura, usually contagious to others around them.
- Probably the least suspecting person you would physically think is a psychopath.

Facade Personality:

- Quite social and has a good amount of friends due to their friendliness.
- Smart and does well in school, typically the role model to others.
- Can sometimes act embarrassed or shy when others are talking about them
- Generally kind hearted to everyone and loves helping out others.
- Bold and adventurous, willing to do things others wouldn't do.
- Overall just a very nice person with a near perfect personality anyone can vibe with.

Yandere Form

Physical Traits/Characteristics:

- Hazy and dark facial expressions or gazes when they get jealous or irritated.

- Dilated or constricted eyes that reveal their true intentions and psychoticness, sometimes accompanied by eye twitching.
- A scary grin and smile due to their delusions and insanity.
- Physical body gestures that show infatuation over their love interest.
- Erratic speeches and yelling usually when the subject is about their love interest.
- High pitched hair raising laughter.
- Lack of feeling and cognitive functions due to the rush adrenaline.

Yandere Personality:

- Prone to highly dangerous mood swings from nice to irrational.
- Infatuated over their love interest.
- Overly confident especially in their skills and thinking ability.
- Gets easily jealous and very overprotective of their love interest
- Delusional when it comes to their love
- Willing to kill and dispose of others if necessary.
- If they do murder others, they will enjoy and laugh at those who they murdered.

Understanding Yandere Lovers: Yanderes and Appeal

- Pretends that their Yandere personality does not exist and will typically deny it.

Do understand that these are just general characteristics and can differ from person to person. Knowing these characteristics beforehand slightly increases your chance of survival, as you would know who to avoid. Coincidentally, this list also helps you understand if you exhibit characteristics of a Yandere. If a majority of these traits resemble your personality, then you are most likely a Yandere.

Yandere Intensity Graph

In order to approximate a Yanderes intensity and craziness, we have to use the **Yandere Intensity Graph**. The Yandere Intensity Graph is used to approximate how crazy a Yandere can get on a combined 1-10 scale. Both categories of obsessive and possessive Yandere intensity can be estimated by charting it out on this graph.

In order to simplify it down, we are going to be using the two most common factors as a basis for determining how crazy a Yandere can get. These two factors we are using are appearance and past tragic events. By using these two factors, we are able to judge Yanderes based on **surface level traits** as well as **deep level traits**. When these two are combined, you are able to approximate the amount of craziness out of 10, with 1 being not so crazy while 10 being the maximum amount of craziness.

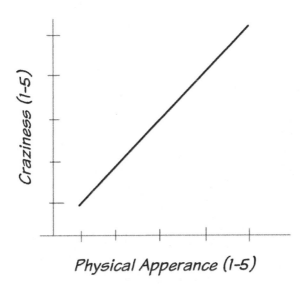

Physical Apperance (1-5)

a. Surface Level Intensity Graph

When it talks about appearance, it is about how good looking a Yandere is as well as their loveable facade personality. In the graph above, you can clearly see the correlation between craziness and appearance. As the Yandere's value of appearance increases, so does the craziness of a Yandere. This is capped at +5 craziness scale

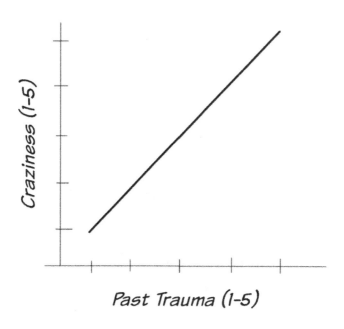

a. Deep Level Intensity Graph

Past tragic events are sometimes hard to scale in the overall scope of things. Scaling past tragic events a Yandere has faced is based on your own discretion on what you consider dark and tragic. As you can see based on the graph, as the Yandere's value of past dark tragic events increases, so does the craziness of a Yandere. This is only natural since this is where a Yandere's personality can mostly develop.

These graphs are particularly useful when determining how intense of a Yandere you would like. All you have to do is add up both craziness determined from the graphs and you should have an accurate Yandere craziness judgement on a 1-10 scale.

Yandere Misconceptions

Due to the nature of a Yandere, many misconceptions arise due to a lack of knowledge and understanding of the Yandere personality. In order to help clear these up, we will be taking a look at some of the more common misconceptions that are held about Yanderes. Learning about their misconceptions has become an essential part in making sure that we understand Yanderes and why they do what they do. Here are some of the common Yandere misconceptions listed below.

Yanderes kill for the fun of it: The reason why Yanderes kill is because of their obsessive or possessive desire for their loved ones. They will never kill without reason or just for the fun of it. I mean their reasoning might be a little distorted or twisted, however, it usually falls in the realm of dealing with their love interest.

They are crazy all the time: As said before, Yanderes both have their crazy personality and their facade personality. This means that they act pretty normal on occasion and when they need to be A majority of the time you will see more of the happy, lovey dovey personality rather than their psychotic states. Their psychotic states only trigger when they have a reason to be jealous, anxious, etc.

Understanding Yandere Lovers: Yanderes and Appeal

Yanderes never stop being Yanderes: Although Yanderes have their personality traits for a good period of their life, this doesn't mean that they won't stop being a Yandere. Once they have found a lover that is truly devoted to loving them back, this is where their Yandere personalities become buried since they would have no reason to act like a Yandere anymore. They can also stop being a Yandere once they have killed their lover or their lover has been killed. At some point, their feelings will typically erode away since they can no longer make any advancements towards their love interest and this usually leads to them either finding a new lover or not loving anyone else.

A Yanderes Public Facade is always fake: In some cases, a Yandere's public facade isn't necessarily fake. This can actually be their true personality given the notion that they have a split personality. This means that if a Yandere has found a lover that loves them back fully, then a majority of the time a Yandere Lover will be experiencing their public facade more than their psychotic personality.

Yanderes always resort to killing: Yanderes don't always have to kill. They will kill only if they really have to. Like previously states, there are other tactics such as manipulation or blackmail that may be more beneficial in getting rid of others without as much consequential reprise.

Yanderes don't think about their actions: Yanderes are

actually those who spend a lot of time thinking things through and making sure of the best possible outcome to get to their goals. Although their actions are mainly driven by their emotions, they will always make sure their actions will benefit them in the long run.

Yanderes will only fall for one person in their lifetime: Although they are depicted as to only love one person throughout their life, this sometimes is not the case. Some Yanderes are just more dedicated than others. Usually, when their love interest dies, they might go the extreme and continue loving them or take some time to mourn them. Eventually they might move on to find a new person to possess/obsess over to fulfill their desire for love.

Yanderes always get their way: Most Yanderes are not Gods. They are everyday people like you and me; maybe with just a little dose of insanity. Since they are very thorough with their actions, they may seem invincible, however, some Yanderes just don't end up getting their way. They often die or get killed in the process due to the results and consequences of their actions. Only a few lucky Yanderes get to keep their love interest with them forever.

Understanding Yandere Lovers: Yanderes and Appeal

Yandere, not Yangire

While on the subject of Yandere misconceptions, one of the biggest ones is the classification of Yangires within the Yandere category. A **Yangire** (ヤンギレ) is an anime/manga character trope meaning cute and psycho. This term describes someone who looks cute and innocent on the outside, but can then snap and turn psychotic at any time. A Yangire usually gets confused or get placed under the category of a Yandere since they both can turn psychotic at any given moment. They are also very similar in the fact that they have some sort of split personality; one being rather normal and one psychotic. This however, does not make a Yangire a Yandere.

Although they are similar and both equally terrifying, they should not be confused. A key difference between that two is that Yangires do not need a love interest as a motivator to turn psychotic. With Yangires, it is typically done on their own accord. In fact, their switch to a different state can happen very randomly and at times don't even need a cause for it to happen. When they go after others, it is normally because of little things such as irritation, a reminder of a past trauma or if they feel like it. They just simply turn crazy without the need of a love interest. This is why Yangires are not Yanderes.

This is a Yangire, not a Yandere!

KAI WEI

How a Yandere Kills

With so much talk about going psychotic, you have to wonder "How does a Yandere kill their target?". A Yandere only kills when they feel as if something/someone threatens their relationship with their love interest. They are psychotic, however, they do not go around killing randomly. This would only make things more complicated for them than it has to be. In fact, if they can, they will mostly use other methods such as injuries, manipulation and blackmail to achieve their desired results. These are known as a **Yanderes Warning Tactics**. Only when it is deemed necessary, will a Yandere decide to kill.

However, when a Yandere makes up their mind on killing, they typically have a certain preference or way of doing it. Most Yanderes tend to kill in a very brutal manner. What matters to them is the suffering you receive before you die. They will make sure that who they are killing regrets their actions by making them suffer. Yanderes will also take pleasure in watching their victim die slowly and painfully. This is why a Yanderes most preferred choice of weapon is either a cutting weapon like a knife or a blunt object like a bat or metal pole to make sure that their victim feels every ounce of pain. Sometimes, Yanderes don't even need a weapon to be able to kill their target. They can use torture devices or even simply push you off a high ledge to get their point across. After their targets have suffered or died, it is usually accompanied by a Yandere's spine-chilling cackle of satisfaction and insanity.

Though their kills tend to be brutal or messy, they are very efficient in clean up and cover up. That is why most of the time, their targets are deemed to be victims of accidents or just end up missing without a trace. The reason they are so tenacious in covering up their murders is because they have to still keep up their public facades as well as not scare off their love interest. They try to reduce any issues with the law or any other parties targeting to threaten their relationship with their love interest. Once they have fully covered up their murders, they will act as if nothing has happened and try their best to divert your attention from it. This cycle of killing and covering up generally continues until there is no one left to compromise a Yanderes relationship with their love interest.

Yandere Power Increase

Yanderes are not just more psychologically intense, they also tend to be more powerful and skilled than the average human being. When fueled by their passion to protect their love interest, they exponentially gain more power in order to achieve their desired intentions, especially when planning to kill. The influx of adrenaline and hormones created by a Yandere are the main reasons for this power up. Their jealousy is one of the biggest triggers that causes this particular increase. This excess power can clearly be seen seeping through a Yanderes aura when they are overcome with bloodlust and jealousy.

Although the increased power is mainly towards physical strength, it also tends to increases skill/ability and intelligence in a Yandere. One common example in regards to an increase in skill is a Yanderes knife wielding abilities. When a Yandere is in a normal state, their ability to properly wield a knife as a weapon is rather poor, however, when they are in a state of jealousy and bloodlust, their ability to use a knife as a weapon dramatically increases in order to kill off their competitor. Of course, this power increase is only temporary. Yanderes are only able to power up when the issue relates to their love interest. Once their objectives are complete and their jealousy subsides, that is when the power up slowly dissipates.

In order for us to calculate the total power increase of a Yandere, here is a simple formula known as the **Yandere Power Formula** which you can use to help you determine how much more powerful a Yandere becomes in their psychotic state.

$$TP = (2.5BP + 1.7S + 1.3INT) * EI$$

TP - Total Power Increase
BP - Base Power Level
S - Skill Power Level
INT - Intelligence Power Level
EI - Emotional Intensity

As you can see with the formula above, the Base, Skill and Intelligence power levels will always be multiplied by a factor of 2.5, 1.7 and 1.3 respectively, no matter the intensity. Depending on the situation, a Yanderes emotional intensity can also factor in the increase in power. EI is capped at level 5 intensity as this is the max a Yandere can multiply their combined total power. Also, another thing to note is that their power is derived mostly on the typical base power levels. This means that if the initial power of the Yandere is high, then it will also be increased to a higher level than those with a weaker base power. As a disclaimer, this formula is meant to accurately portray human Yanderes and not other beings such as gods and animals.

A Yandere's Power can be seen seeping through their dark aura.

Why would a Yandere like you?

Now you may be wondering, "Why would a Yandere like me in the first place?", "Is there any way to really prevent them liking me?" Well to tell you the truth, there is very little you can really do avoid this. There is the option of living a secluded lifestyle away from society, however, that just isn't the most feasible lifestyle for anyone. Like everyone else, their development of love for you is something that occurs naturally. Although their development of love for you is something that is completely out of your control, there are certain traits or actions that increase your probability of becoming loved by a Yandere.

Childhood Backstory: A very common way for a Yandere to develop feelings for you is through being a part of their childhood. Our childhood memories are very powerful, and we tend to get attached to other people at an early age. Even if you completely forgot about those memories, to a Yandere, those early moments created a lifelong attachment that simply developed over the years towards their pursuit for you.

Being Weak/Helpless: They say that opposites attract, and this is especially true when a Yandere develops feelings for someone else. Their facade personality is typically very sociable and can be seen as a role model in societal groups. Due to this facade, they tend to look for those who are opposite from themselves such as those who are secluded and usually not part of a big social group. This also makes it easier for a Yandere since they don't have to deal with lots of other people trying to go after the same love interest.

Savior Complex: The **savior complex** is a term used to describe a situation where someone falls in love with you when you save them. This does not necessarily have to be life/death situations, however, for Yanderes, simple things such as trying to protect them from bullies or helping them when they are struggling can lead them to loving you. This is especially effective for attracting Obsessive Yanderes even if you are not aware that you have triggered someone's savior complex.

Initial Infatuation: Like everyone else, people can naturally become attracted to you based on your physical appearance or personality. Yanderes who develop love via **initial infatuation** typically start off as an Obsessive Yandere. They at first love you because they are naturally attracted to you. From here they dive deeper into their delusions over their love for you until their infatuation turns more into an obsession. If you become aware of this early, you can simply disappear or move somewhere further away to avoid their love for you. The only reason you can do this at an early stage is because their obsession for you isn't quite as strong yet due to the lack of time and development.

*Please note that these actions/traits also attract other types of people and not just Yanderes. Yanderes simply have a higher preference for people that have these actions/traits, which in turn leads to the higher probability of a Yandere liking you.

I knew we would be together ever since we were kids...

What makes a Yandere Attractive?

Now this is the big question! If Yanderes are so crazy and scary, why are there still groups of people who have some kind of attraction toward them? In hindsight, it seems a bit unreasonable for anyone to like someone so psychotic. Despite all this, there are is still a niche group known as **Yandere Lovers** who truly love the personality traits of a Yandere. Although it might seem strange to like a Yandere personality, Yandere Lovers do have logical reasons for their attraction towards Yanderes. Below are the 5 reasons why Yandere Lovers love the Yandere personality.

1. A Strong and Confident Lover

2. Masochistic Desire

3. Allure of Fear

4. Yandere Lover's Insecurity

5. True Devotion to Love

In order to truly understand Yandere Lovers, we will be taking an in-depth look at these reasons in the next couple pages.

A Strong and Confident Lover

One of the reasons that Yanderes are attractive to some people is the fact that they are strong and confident lovers. What I mean by this is that they are the type to take the lead and take the reins in a relationship. Yanderes are confident and actively make the first move. They know exactly what they want out of the relationship as well as do what it takes to achieve that goal. You would no longer have to make any of the plans and Yanderes would gladly be the one in charge.

These traits of a Yandere can be attractive to some people, especially those who tend to act very passive when they are in a relationship with someone. In order to fulfill these desired personality traits, people will start to gain affection towards a Yandere, despite them being possessive/obsessive. The big tradeoff is that you will typically have no control or freewill in the things you want to do in a relationship. For some people like Yandere Lovers, that is completely fine.

You will notice that your Yandere will always know what they want.

Masochistic Desire

As crazy as it may seem, some people might see Yanderes as potential lovers due to their own personal Masochistic Desires. Derived from the term masochist, a **Masochistic Desire** is a desire for sexual gratification through pain or humiliation. In our context, the pain and humiliation would come from Yanderes. This desire can commonly be fulfilled in the form of restrictions, manipulation and even torture. In the case of Yandere Lovers, their desires can either be fulfilled in one of two ways. One of the ways is through a simple request. Since a Yandere would be willing to do anything for you, they would gladly accept your request of fulfilling your Masochistic Desires, especially if it turns you on. The other way is through **Deliberate Yandere Manipulation**. This is where you purposely do things to anger or make your Yandere jealous in order to release their Yandere personality. Of course the danger of this would be if you did it often and frequently enough, it will end up resulting in your death/demise.

Although it is true that Yanderes can inflict pain or humiliation to their love interest, it is not as common as you would think. Yanderes do love you and therefore would rarely do anything to hurt you unless deemed necessary. It will end up varying from Yandere to Yandere on how they will react to any Masochistic Desires you may have.

Of course, masochism isn't for everyone...

Allure of Fear

Fear can be a powerful aphrodisiac to others, especially for Yandere Lovers. This **Allure of Fear** thus creates an initial attraction towards Yanderes. A Yanderes actions of being possessive or obsessive can stimulate these sexual desire due to the fear it causes them to feel. Since fear is not typically generated in a normal relationship, Yandere Lovers look towards Yanderes in order to receive their fear stimulus.

Now there is nothing wrong with this. I mean this is similar to watching scary movies in order to feel the excitement that you wouldn't normally feel in their everyday life. The only problem with the Allure of Fear when going after a Yandere is that, it can only act as the initial stimulus. After multiple exposures to fear from a Yandere, it will end up causing you to become desensitized and look for a new partner to receive that same feeling. And you should know by now how leaving a Yandere can cause some unwanted events to occur in your life.

Fear can bring pleasure to others.

Yandere Lover's Insecurity

Yandere Lovers Insecurity is a big issue that Yandere Lovers would like resolved. This is the large amount of insecurities one has whenever they are in a relationship with someone, due to their lack of confidence and trust in their partner. One way of resolving this would be having a Yandere as a romantic partner. Since a Yandere would never want to leave their partners side, there would really be no room for Yandere Lovers to be insecure about their relationship. This is what is most comforting to those insecure Yandere Lovers.

Even though Yanderes can either be more possessive or obsessive, it is merely a small price to pay in order to receive this comfort. Insecurity is something we all will deal with from time to time, however, knowing that you have a Yandere, it is one less thing you would have to worry about in a relationship. Of course, Lover's Insecurity can also be resolved through other tactics with less harmful repercussion. Having a Yandere is just a more of a rapid way of gaining immediate results.

If you are insecure, Yanderes will always make time

True Devotion to Love

This last reason is probably the most influential part of why a Yandere Lover would love a Yandere. A Yandere's devotion to love their partner can never compare to anyone else. What you receive from them is known as **True Yandere Love**. This is love achieved at the highest level, which is only possible due to a Yandere's possessive/obsessive personality trope. Aside from the craziness that Yanderes bring in, it can be viewed as great to have someone that loves you that much. To some people, it might be seen as being loved too much. For Yandere Lovers, this is a longing they wish to have in a relationship. It might be restrictive at times, but who wouldn't want unconditional and limitless love from their significant other?

Yandere Lover's Fallacy

Besides the Yandere personality, one of the biggest issues that a Yandere lover has to face is known as the Yandere Lover's Fallacy. The **Yandere Lover's Fallacy** states that those who truly love a Yandere for their personality type will eventually lose interest since the Yandere will have no reason to exhibit the traits that initially infatuated a Yandere lover. Simply stated, a Yandere Lover's love cannot truly exist when they are together with a Yandere. This leads to the cycle of falling in and out of love with a Yandere, thus making it impossible for a Yandere Lover to ever truly love a Yandere. It is a bit ironic isn't it? There are however, two ways you can avoid this fallacy.

A preventative measure to stop this fallacy from occurring in the first place is by not falling deeply in love with your Yandere. Instead, you would be placing yourself at a middle ground where it would still satisfy your desires of having a Yandere, yet not fully committing to their love. This may be hard for some people since the main issue of this is that you would constantly have to go in and out of a Yandere's wrath while trying your best in making sure you or others don't get killed in the process. Also, if your Yandere ever found out that you have been playing them like this, then you should already know that dire consequences are sure to follow. If you are willing to do this, you are just as crazy as a Yandere for living life so close to the edge.

The easier alternative is the post-preventative measure. This measure is to learn to love the different aspects of the person that are separate from the Yandere personality. Once you fall in love with your Yandere, after a while, you will learn your Yandere's true personality that is separate from the facade as well as the Yandere personality. This post-preventative measure works out if you happen to be compatible with your Yandere outside the spectrum of the Yandere personality. If not then, there is no other known way to combat the Yandere Lover's Fallacy. This is why the Yandere Lover's Fallacy is every Yandere Lover's greatest dilemma.

KAI WEI

Yandere Lover's Creed

If you find yourself having an attraction towards a Yandere after all this, As a Yandere Lover you are dedicated to loving Yanderes. In order to become a true Yandere Lover, you must understand and recite this creed to remind you of your love for Yanderes as well as your purpose in life.

I am a Yandere Lover.

I say this proudly with no shame as this is who I truly am.

With my love and dedication, I shall continue to love Yanderes with an open heart as well as an open mind.

I will live to serve and love Yanderes

Even if they may not love me in return.

May I forever support their effort and be inspired by their passions

As they drive myself to love them even more.

I am drawn to their beauty and insanity

As it stimulates and aspires me to have a Yandere of my own.

I will accept the consequences of my actions and am willing to die for my Yandere.

Without a Yandere to love, I am meaningless and have no other purpose in life

By my power I swear.

To always love Yanderes until they are no more.

X_____

Conclusion

Yanderes are complex creatures and are definitely not for everyone. As a disclaimer, I would like to say that you should pursue them at your own risk. If you currently have a Yandere loving you, well, I wish you good luck and hope you don't fuck up. I hope you were able to enjoy and learn more about Yanderes and I applaud you for making it to the end of this book. I may not have covered every little niche about Yanderes, however, that journey is something you must take and experience if you wish to learn more. This book is merely a helping hand and you must decide for yourself if Yanderes are right for you. Thank you again for choosing to read this book and I hope that one day, this book will become of some service to you.

Best Regards,
Kai Wei

Glossary

Allure of Fear - Fear can be a powerful aphrodisiac to others and the allure of fear is made when someone wants to receive fear from a relationship.

Artificial Yandere - someone who chooses to become a Yandere out of their own free will and develops their traits artificially over time.

Deep level traits - traits that truly define what a person is like on the inside. This is not normally seen unless you are close to someone.

Deliberate Yandere Manipulation - is where you purposely do things to anger or make your Yandere jealous in order to release their Yandere personality.

Facade form - a separate personality that enables them to hide their true Yandere intentions from others and have a completely normal one as a facade.

Initial Infatuation - a term used to describe the natural liking of someone due to their physical appearance or personality.

Masochistic Desire - a desire for sexual gratification through pain or humiliation.

Natural Yandere - someone who develops into a Yandere due to natural experiences and circumstances, typically out of their control.

Obsessive Yanderes - those who obsess over their future together with their love interest and their actions are done to make sure that happens.

Personality disorder - is a type of mental condition that often leads to harmful patterns of thinking, behaving and basic interactions.

Possessive Yanderes - are those whose actions and beliefs are directed towards keeping their love interests as theirs, and theirs alone.

Rejection alteration - Due to the influx of various negative thoughts and emotions after a rejection, they go through a state of denial

Savior complex - a term used to describe a situation where someone falls in love with you when you save them.

Surface level traits - physical traits normally displayed by a person to the public.

True Yandere Love - This is love achieved at the highest level, which is only possible due to a Yandere's possessive/obsessive personality trope.

Tsundere - an anime/manga slang word that is used to describe a character trait that switches between the two emotional states of hostility and affection.

Tsundere Maturity Stage - where a Tsundere in a sense, "matures" psychologically as the shock, sadness and the pain of rejection, shapes their current personality and helps them better comprehend their emotions.

Yandere - A person who at first seems caring, sweet and innocent, however, they turn to someone obsessive, violent and psychotic often due to their devotion towards their particular love interest.

Yandere Intensity Graph - used to approximate how crazy a Yandere can get on a combined 1-10 scale.

Yandere Lovers - A niche group of people who truly love the personality traits of a Yandere.

Understanding Yandere Lovers: Yanderes and Appeal

Yandere Lovers Insecurity - is the large amount of insecurities one has whenever they are in a relationship with someone, due to their lack of confidence and trust in their partner.

Yandere Lover's Fallacy - states that those who truly love a Yandere for what they are will eventually lose interest since the Yandere will have no reason to exhibit the traits that initially infatuated a Yandere lover.

Yandere Power Formula - a formula used to help you determine how much more powerful a Yandere becomes in their psychotic state.

Yanderes Warning Tactics - methods such as injuries, manipulation and blackmail to achieve their desired results without the use of murder or killing.

Yangire - describes someone who looks cute and innocent on the outside, but can then snap and turn psychotic at any time.

KAI WEI

Made in United States
Orlando, FL
01 June 2024